EXPRESS DIESEL TRAINS

GEORGE WOODS

AMBERLEY

First published 2023

Amberley Publishing
The Hill, Stroud
Gloucestershire, GL5 4EP

www.amberley-books.com

Copyright © George Woods, 2023

The right of George Woods to be identified as
the Author of this work has been asserted in
accordance with the Copyrights, Designs and
Patents Act 1988.

ISBN 978 1 3981 1564 4 (print)
ISBN 978 1 3981 1565 1 (ebook)

British Library Cataloguing in Publication Data.
A catalogue record for this book is available from
the British Library.

Origination by Amberley Publishing.
Printed in the UK.

Introduction

In August 1968, after over 150 years of service, British Rail withdrew the last steam locomotives from everyday use, and the changeover to diesel and electric power was complete.

In reality, many services were much the same. The timings on many main line routes had become quicker after dieselisation, especially on the WCML which had been electrified from London to Birmingham, Liverpool and Manchester, resulting in a huge improvement not only in speed but also frequency. The ECML from London to Leeds, Newcastle and Edinburgh had seen big improvements with the introduction of the Deltic diesels, but in general many lagged behind, especially the cross-country routes. These compared poorly to services in other parts of Europe, whose railways were being electrified on a large scale with the resulting improvements in journey times and service frequencies.

While British Rail struggled to get government approval for modernisation schemes, the French railways (SNCF) were being influenced by the Japanese Shinkansen high speed train, and since 1966 had been developing a national high speed rail network known as the TGV – Train à Grande Vitesse, or high speed train. This was first developed as a gas turbine train, but was soon changed to electric power after the 1973 oil crisis. The first line from Paris to Lyon opened in 1981 with trains travelling at up to 300 kph, and by 2011 the route milage had expanded to 2700 km serving nearly all the large French cities and connecting into neighbouring countries as well.

Since the advent of the TGV many other European countries have constructed and introduced high speed rail services and now most European major cities are connected not only internally but internationally as well. The only high speed line that runs in the UK is HS1, which opened in late 2007 connecting London to Paris and Brussels via the Channel Tunnel – and this only came into being after much reluctance by governments of the time.

In the 1970s BR was also developing a high speed train, the APT-E, which was also gas turbine-powered and on trials reached a speed of 152.3 mph, but as the French discovered the fuel crisis of the mid-1970s made it uneconomical, so development was halted in 1976. An electric version, the advanced passenger train that was designed to tilt to allow higher speeds on the curvaceous WCML, was being developed and reached a speed of 162 mph on test, but ran into many problems with the tilting mechanism and after suffering embarrassing publicity was shelved through lack of funds in 1985.

Luckily, at the same time a diesel train capable of running at 125 mph, a development of the Midland Pullman (a six-car diesel train with a power car at each end), was introduced on the Manchester to St Pancras service in 1960. A prototype train was built at Derby and Crewe and started trials in 1972, during which a top speed of 143 mph was reached, resulting in ninety-five trains being put into service on most of British Rail's front line services. The original 125 was given a makeover by industrial designer Kenneth Grange, who was originally asked to design the livery but also redesigned the shape of the power cars that have since become a design icon.

Much work was needed on both the Western Region routes and the ECML to allow the higher speeds before the InterCity 125, as it became known, could be introduced. The 125 began running on the Paddington to Bristol and South Wales routes in 1976, and came into ECML service in 1978. The CrossCountry routes from Scotland and northern England to the south coast and West Country were next, plus services from Paddington to Devon and Cornwall in 1981. The trains were an instant success with the public, with passenger numbers increasing wherever they were introduced.

Initially the 125s for the Western Region services consisted of a Class 253 (later to become Class 43) power car at each end equipped with a 2250 hp Paxman Valenta engine, four second class coaches, a buffet car and two first class coaches. In 1978 the first sets for the ECML were introduced and were similar, except for the inclusion of an extra second class coach. From 1979 125s were put to work on services from Paddington to Plymouth and Penzance, with the last services to get 125s being the CrossCountry routes in 1981, and the Midland Mainline from St Pancras to Sheffield and Nottingham, which began in 1982.

In the 1990s British Rail was privatised, and the companies that took over services worked by 125s made several important alterations including the replacement of the Paxman Valenta engines, which were becoming worn out, with the MTU 4000 2720 kw engine used from 2005 onwards. All the companies refurbished the passenger accommodation, and in 2002 GNER added another second class coach to their ECML 125s to ease overcrowding.

In 2007 Grand Central Railway, an open access TOC originally set up in 2000, introduced a new service from Sunderland to Kings Cross using some of the last 125s powered by Valenta engines. These 125s were not in the best of shape, and for the first few months the service suffered from train failures. In 2010 two Class 180 units were leased and entered service on their new London to Bradford route, and by 2017 all the IC125 sets were transferred to East Midland Trains with all services now operated by ten refurbished Class 180s.

The Class 180 Adelante trains have had quite a chequered career; they are the only DMUs anywhere to operate with diesel-hydraulic transmission, and fourteen five-car sets were ordered from Alstom by First Great Western to operate at speeds up to 125 mph on increased services to South Wales with the first trains entering service in late 2001. The trains suffered many problems in service, eventually being placed on less important routes, and being returned to the leasing company between 2007 and 2009. They were then used by Hull Trains on their services from Hull to London, but again reliability problems have seen them replaced by the new Class 802 bi-powered trains. Northern Rail had two for service on their Manchester to Blackpool route until 2011, and East Midlands Railway have four in service until they get new Class 810s in 2023.

In 2001 Virgin CrossCountry introduced the 125 mph Class 220 Voyager four-car DMU into service, and a total of thirty-four sets were built by Bombardier with each coach powered by a Cummins 750 hp diesel engine driving a generator to power the traction motors. At the same time forty-four Class 221s were introduced, the main differences from the 220 being that they consist of five coaches and have a tilting mechanism to allow higher speed around curves, although this has never been used.

In 2006 the franchise was put out to tender again and won by Arriva Trains, who have run services since then and will keep the franchise until 2023. They retained the Class 220 and 221 Voyager trains, and also obtained some 125 HST sets to ease overcrowding. XC is responsible for the UK's longest through service, which runs from Aberdeen to Penzance, plus all of the long-distance routes from north to south that do not pass through London.

The Class 222, which is very similar to the Class 220 and 221, came into service in 2004 with Midland Main Line services from St Pancras to Derby, Nottingham and Sheffield. Also powered by Cummins 750 hp diesel engines are twenty-seven four- and nine-car sets that were built and entered service in 2004. These services are now run by East Midland Trains.

In 2012 the Department for Transport announced that Hitachi would be awarded the contract to develop and build the replacement trains for the IC125 and 225 fleets, which were to be made at a new facility in Newton Aycliffe County Durham. The first of the new 800 series trains are powered from the 25kv overhead line, with underfloor diesel engines for running on non-electrified routes, first entered service with GWR in 2017 and with LNER in late 2018. Other operators are Hull Trains, TransPennine Express and Lumo.

Amazingly the IC125 lasted in service until 2019, being replaced on GWR and LNER services by the bi-powered 800 series trains, but both GWR and Scotrail are running refurbished short formation four- and five-car sets on some of their services, so they will be around for some time yet.

HS2 is now under construction from London to Birmingham, with extensions to Sheffield and Leeds with a link to the ECML serving Newcastle and Scotland. All this should, of course, have happened forty years ago, but unfortunately our politicians are too short-sighted to look beyond the next general election. Better late than never?

Abbreviations
APT-E: Advanced Passenger Train - Experimental
BR: British Rail
DMU: Diesel Multiple Unit
ECML: East Coast Main Lines
GC: Grand Central
GNER: Great North Eastern Railway
GWR: Great Western Railways
LNER: London North Eastern Railway
MTU: Motoren-und Turbinen-Union
NRM: National Railway Museum
SNCF: Société nationale des chemins de fer français
TOC: Train Operating Company
WCML: West Coast Main Line
XC: Cross Country
VTCC: Virgin Trains CrossCountry

Locomotion No.1 and the prototype HST seen at the exhibition held at Shildon to mark the 150th anniversary of the opening of the Stockton and Darlington Railway. 28 August 1975.

One of the Western Pullman trains departs from Paddington in May 1969 with a late afternoon service. At this time the original blue and white livery was being replaced by the BR Corporate scheme of blue and grey.

On 27 April 1973, just a week before the service finished, the Bristol Pullman speeds towards Paddington on the last part of its journey, and is seen passing the Southall water tower (also known as Southall Castle), which was finished in 1903 and is now a Grade II listed building . The large gasholder in the background was not so lucky, being demolished in 2019.

Above and below: Two pictures of the first 125 train I travelled on in August 1976, journeying from Paddington to Reading. The leading power car was 253 007 (43014), and bringing up the rear was 253 006 (43012). They are seen leaving Reading station heading west to Bristol.

253 009 (43019) is brand new from Crewe Works, and is seen at York station on 11 July 1976 on a test run that will make use of the high speed stretch of line to Darlington, where it will be able to run at 125 mph.

253 012 waits for its passengers at Paddington station before departing for Bristol on a Sunday morning. 27 May 1977.

Above and below: Two pictures taken on 13 June 1977 of what I believe to be the first visit of an InterCity 125 to Kings Cross. The occasion was the journey from Gleneagles to London on a specially commissioned Western Region 125 carrying the delegates who had attended the Commonwealth Heads of Government Conference that had been held at the Gleneagles Hotel. The train was formed of unit 253 026 but included extra catering vehicles. The pictures show the train in platform 1 after arrival, and the empty stock departing for Old Oak Common.

253 027 catches a sunny spell approaching Didcot with a westbound service, just beating a rain shower sweeping in from the east in September 1977.

On 1 March 1979 the Western Region allowed 6000 *King George V* to make its first journey from Paddington since the end of steam in 1965. The exit from Paddington was made alongside this immaculate HST 253 006, which of course raced ahead and is seen passing Southall MPD long before KG5 got to us. Unfortunately it all went pear-shaped later in the day, as at Didcot KG5 was found to have a hot axle box and could not make the return journey.

254 008 is seen passing Hitchin on the 8 May 1978, with the first Flying Scotsman service for Kings Cross. Note the lack of catering vehicles.

A Harrogate to Kings Cross HST leaves Weeton Tunnel, and heads for Arthington Viaduct and Leeds. 20 October 1979.

Above and below: Two pictures at Dringhouses, which lies just south of York. Above, 254 003 passes a busy looking Dringhouses Yard in June 1979 with a train for Kings Cross. The yard closed in 1987 and is now a large housing estate. Below, 254 007 has charge of another Kings Cross train, captured from the sports field south of the bridge.

HST power car 43064 passes the NRM at York in December 1979 with an HST barrier vehicle, probably after receiving attention at Heaton TMD.

254 015 is about to pass under the Water End road bridge at Clifton with a northbound service on a misty afternoon in December 1979. Above the train is the York Civil Engineers Depot, and the sidings for the York Carriage Works can be seen to the right.

The changing scene at Newcastle Central on 6 June 1981 as an HST departs for London, shortly to be followed by 55014 on the Edinburgh to Plymouth train.

Just to the south another HST crosses the King Edward VII Bridge on the approach to Newcastle station. The bridge, designed by Charles Harrison, was opened in 1906 and carries the railway 112 feet above the River Tyne.

Above and below: Two pictures taken in Gateshead on 6 June 1981. Above, 43058 leads an HST crossing the High Level bridge over the River Tyne and through Gateshead station on its way south to Kings Cross. This is unusual as southbound trains usually cross over the King Edward VII Bridge. Designed by Robert Stephenson, the double-deck bridge carries a roadway under the railway deck. It was opened in 1849, and carries the railway 120 feet above the river. Below, a southbound HST with 43056 at the rear accelerates away from King Edward South Junction towards Team Valley and Durham.

Two pictures of the northbound Flying Scotsman HST passing through Selby station in October 1981, with 43113 leading and 43063 at the rear. Because of mining subsidence in the area, it was decided to build a new line avoiding Selby, and on 3 October 1983 the Selby Diversion was opened allowing ECML services to run at 125 mph between Doncaster and York.

On a snowy day in January 1982, a northbound HST speeds through Peterborough station. For many years the station here stood on a sharp curve that restricted speed to 20 mph, and it was not until 1972 that it was completely rebuilt, allowing 100 mph running.

In May 1980 the Rocket 150 celebrations were held at Rainhill to mark 150 years since George Stephenson's *Rocket* locomotive won the competition that would start the Railway Age. Among the exhibits taking part was this brand-new InterCity 125, seen here with power car W43137 leading the train past the crowds of spectators.

A Bristol to Paddington HST departs from Westbury station past a typical ex-GWR semaphore signal and signal box in June 1983.

Above and below: Two pictures taken north of York. Above, 253 028 is running at over 100 mph near Tollerton with the Plymouth to Edinburgh CrossCountry service in August 1984. Below, in August 1985 a southbound HST runs down the Up slow near Shipton, as the fast lines were closed for maintenance.

The southbound Flying Scotsman crosses the Royal Border Bridge at Berwick-upon-Tweed on its way from Edinburgh to London in September 1984. The twenty-eight-arch bridge carries the railway 121 feet above the River Tweed, and was opened in 1850 by Queen Victoria.

Two HSTs await departure from Kings Cross on a sunny morning in November 1985. Both wear different liveries; on the left, 43064 *City of York* is in the InterCity Executive livery and the other is still in the original livery.

Above and below: Two pictures of 125s at Holgate just prior to arriving at York station in January 1986. First 43030 is on a CrossCountry train, followed by an InterCity service from Kings Cross to Edinburgh. The Holgate Road bridge, seen in the lower picture, was built in 1911 and was raised in 1985 to allow space for the overhead wires for the ECML electrification.

Above and below: Two pictures of East Coast 125s passing at York station on a bright January day in 1986. 43055 is on the rear of the northbound train. The southbound unit has the driver's newspaper acting as a temporary blind.

Above and below: Back to Holgate for two pictures of a 125 in the InterCity Executive livery, captured in December 1986. A northbound train gets stopped at the signal and waits for its platform to become vacant. The leading power car is 43051, and at the rear is 43113 *City of Newcastle Upon Tyne*. This immaculate set would seem to be in its first day of service after passing through Derby works for overhaul and a full repaint.

Above and below: Two pictures of 43155 *BBC Look North* taken at York station. Above, the loco is seen in April 1987 and shows it leading a train for Kings Cross arriving at platform 9 with the coaches still in the original livery. Below, a close-up taken in November 1989 showing the weather-beaten paintwork that is the result of the 1,000 miles or so that trains covered each day.

Above and below: One of the problems with the HST was the exhaust staining on the top of the driver's cab, which became worse after the cowling was fitted over the exhaust. Several attempts were made, including this one tried on 43038 that involved painting the roof white – it didn't exactly solve the problem! The top image was taken at Leeds in May 1990, and the lower image at York in July 1991.

43079 climbs through Heeley on its way out of Sheffield with a train for St Pancras in September 1991.

Later the same day, 43054 stands in Sheffield station alongside an impressive floral display, awaiting departure time and also heading for London.

For a while in 1990 there was an unusual working that started from Neville Hill depot in Leeds and ran empty to Newcastle to form a southbound service. 43040 is seen in May 1990 on this train, which was booked to take the freight avoiding line instead of running through York station. To the right is the Clifton Civil Engineers depot, and the line of coaches to the left of the HST are waiting entry to the York Carriage Works, which closed in 1992.

An experimental HST set approaches Colton Junction in September 1990. I believe this was in connection with trials of the coaches for the Channel Tunnel Nightstar trains.

Above and below: Two pictures taken near Chesterfield on 29 September 1990. Above, 43050 departs with a St Pancras to Sheffield train showing the Church of St Mary and All Saints with its famous crooked spire in the background. Below, a southbound train for London has just passed Tapton Junction and approaches the station.

43023 waits to depart from Carlisle station with the Penzance to Glasgow train in October 1991.

43054 is on the rear of the Hertfordshire Railtours Cumbrian Coast 125 Tour on 25 April 1992. The train has just passed through Grange Over Sands station and will shortly cross the River Kent viaduct at Arnside.

43065 leads the 09.50 Glasgow to Penzance service through Waitby. it has been diverted over the Settle & Carlisle line in April 1993.

Taking its normal route over Shap, 43070 speeds the Glasgow to Penzance train through Greenholme. 16 July 1996.

43006 passes the site of Brent station with a Paddington to Penzance train on 12 July 1996. The station, which was the junction for the Kingsbridge branch, closed on 5 October 1964.

43105, resplendent in its new GNER livery, pauses at York station during its journey to Edinburgh on 8 April 1997. GNER was owned by Sea Containers Ltd and operated services until 2007, when the company went bankrupt.

Above and below: Two pictures taken at Sheffield station on 8 April 1997. Above, Midland Mainline 43059 awaits departure time for St Pancras, and below 43093 *York Festival 88* looks very colourful in its new Virgin CrossCountry livery while working a Newcastle to Bristol service.

43100 passes Low Gill with the Glasgow to Penzance train on 3 May 1997. The M6 motorway can be seen beyond the end of the train, with the Howgill Fells towering in the background.

In June 1998 an unidentified HST dodges the showers as it approaches Colton Junction, just south of York, with a northbound CrossCountry service.

Above and below: Two pictures taken near Colton Junction of Virgin CrossCountry HSTs on southbound services to the west of England. Above, 43099 is seen in June 1998, and, below, 43180 brings up the rear on 20.11.99.

Above and below: Two pictures taken at St Pancras of Midland Main Line HSTs in February 1999. Above, a line up of three units at the buffer stops, and, below, 43054 is waiting to depart for Sheffield. The station is looking shabby having survived plans to demolish it in the 1960s and has not had much attention since. But all is about to change for the better with the complete rebuilding as the London Terminal for the HS1 services to Paris and Brussels via the Channel Tunnel, which opened in November 2007.

Express Diesel Trains

43007 powers past Greenholme on the climb up to Shap Summit with the Penzance to Glasgow service on 8 June 2000.

Above and below: Two pictures of the Glasgow to Penzance train approaching Blea Moor signal box with 43104 and 43092 diverted via the Settle & Carlisle line because of engineering work on the WCML on 23 March 2002. Above, the train after it has left Blea Moor Tunnel. Below, it is seen with the 2372-foot Ingleborough just visible through the haze in the background.

Three pictures taken at Reading on 17 April 2002. Above, 43025 *Exeter* arriving with a train for Paddington. Middle, 43029 on another Paddington train. Below, 43176 is also Paddington bound with 166 218 on the middle road, and a westbound HST departing.

An unusual pairing at York station in July 2000, with 43197 on a northbound ECML service and 373 3311 on a service to Kings Cross. The Eurostar was one of five sets on loan to GNER to ease a shortage of trains.

Two Virgin CrossCountry HSTs pass at the north end of York station on 13 August 2002.

43013 arrives at Derby on 29 April 2000 with a northbound VTCC train. The clock tower in the background belongs to the surviving part of the former Midland Railway workshops.

Also at Derby, 43094 prepares to depart for the south with a Mark II coach in tow on 21 April 2002.

43158 *Dartmoor the Pony Express* heads a VTCC service approaching Colton Junction on 10 May 2003.

43099 stands in Carlisle station with a southbound VTCC train on 10 June 2003.

A view of the west end of Edinburgh Waverley station taken in June 2001 with a Virgin HST departing on the left, and a GNER train at far right. No fewer than seventeen buses are visible on the bridges that cross the station, and the world famous Balmoral Hotel, formerly the North British Hotel, with its clock tower, dominates the scene with the remaining part of Calton Jail to its right.

43120 waits to leave Aberdeen station with the North Briton service to Leeds on 26 June 2003.

43157 had worked the last VTCC service on 27 September 2003, and is seen here in debranded Virgin colours at Sheffield on 24 April 2004 with a northbound service.

Also on 24 April 2004, 43043 *Leicester County Cricket Club*, on a Midland Mainline train to St Pancras, has a change of driver at Derby.

Above and below: Two pictures taken at Kings Cross on 2 June 2004 when GNER were responsible for the ECML services. Above, 43116 *City of Kingston Upon Hull* is surrounded by Class 91s. Below, 43105 *City of Inverness* brings up the rear of a northbound departure entering Gasworks Tunnel.

Above and below: Two pictures at Reading on 3 June 2004 during the time First were running Great Western services from Paddington. Above, 43169 *The National Trust* heads towards London as 43016 runs in with a westbound service. Below, we witness a ritual held during many stations stops as the power cars were notorious for dirtying the windscreens with their exhaust, which needed frequent cleaning, here 43016 gets attention.

An HST makes for Paddington through the Sonning Cutting on 3 June 2004. Opened in 1840, and up to 60 feet deep, the cutting lies about 2 miles east of Reading on Brunel's Great Western main line from London to Bristol.

43062 is one of the power cars on Network Rail's New Measurement Train, and is seen at the Crewe Works Open Day on 10 September 2005.

For a short time in 2003/4 Midland Mainline ran a service, known as Project Rio, from St Pancras to Manchester during major works on the WCML route to Euston. 43161 waits to leave Manchester Piccadilly on 2 July 2004.

43082 waits to depart from Derby for London on 22 April 2006. Midland Mainline services became part of the East Midland franchise in 2007.

43114 *East Riding of Yorkshire* is about to depart from York with the North Briton Leeds to Aberdeen service on 15 October 2005.

43039 waits to head south from York station at 13.55 with a Kings Cross train on 12 September 2006.

Right and below: Two views of the Highland Chieftain service from Kings Cross to Inverness on 12 September 2006. 43106 *Fountains Abbey* departs from York, and at the rear is 43109 *Leeds International Film Festival.* At 581 miles, the journey is the longest through service in the UK, and takes eight hours.

Above and below: Two views of an Aberdeen to London HST taken at Edinburgh Waverley station on 29 December 2006. Above, passengers throng on platform 2, and below the train departs on time at 15.00, as shown by the clock on the Balmoral Hotel.

43314 *East Riding of Yorkshire* departs from York on 18 September 2007 with a northbound train, taken from the viewing platform at the NRM.

43092 and 43182 wait to take up their next duties at Bristol Temple Meads station on 22 February 2008.

43089 *Hayabusa* heads the Network Rail Measurement Train out of Birkett Tunnel during its run from Leeds to Carlisle on 19 April 2008.

Above and below: Two pictures taken at York station on 9 May 2008 of a Grand Central service from Kings Cross to Sunderland. Above, 43084 before renumbering and the addition of the orange stripe. It was one of the last HST power cars to retain the Velenta engine. Below, 43166 is at the head of the train in debranded East Midland colours, which had been borrowed to cover a power car shortage.

Above and below: When GNER lost the contract for the ECML in 2007 it was handed to National Express, and these two pictures show one of their services leaving York on 28 May 2008. Above, 43306 in the new owner's East Coast livery. Below, the rear power car 43053 has rebranded GNER colours.

43014 is one of the original power cars that have worked the Network Rail Measurement Train since 2003, and is seen here at Carlisle station on 6 August 2008.

43303 *Craigentinny* waits to depart from Leeds with a service for Kings Cross on 27 May 2009. The train is now wearing the new National Express East Coast livery. Within a few months National Express would default on the franchise.

Above and below: 150 134 departs for Harrogate on 15 July 2013 as a southbound East Coast service arrives at York with 43318 leading and 43309 at rear. This is the 'New' East Coast government-owned operator that ran the trains until Virgin took over in 2014.

Great Western HST power car 43159 stands alongside one of the prototype power cars, 41001, during the Railfest 2012 exhibition at the NRM York on 6 June 2012.

On 1 March 2015, Stagecoach/Virgin took over the East Coast franchise and these two shots show the interim livery with the Virgin logo transposed onto the East Coast colours. Above, 43315 speeds south through Doncaster during a heavy downpour on 7 July 2015. Below, 43295 waits to depart from York with a train for Kings Cross on 5 August 2015.

Above and below: Two pictures of Grand Central HSTs on the London–Wearside service, passing through Doncaster at high speed. Above, 43480 with a Kings Cross to Sunderland train; 180 110 is waiting to follow with a Hull trains service. Below, 43484 speeds south with the midday Sunderland to Kings Cross service on 25 February 2016.

43465 speeds through Doncaster with the midday Grand Central Kings Cross to Sunderland train on 25 February 2016. The Grand Central HSTs were replaced by Class 180 units in 2017.

Above and below: Two pictures of the new Virgin East Coast colour scheme. Above, 43215 departs from Doncaster for Kings Cross on 25 February 2016, and below 43310 has just arrived from the north at the greatly improved Kings Cross station on 17 August 2016. Note the trees visible outside the station – something rarely seen on this part of the Euston Road before!

Above and below: At the country end of Kings Cross, GC 43480 is ready to depart for Sunderland, and across the road at St Pancras 43089 is on an East Midlands service to Sheffield. Compared with the Gothic magnificence of the original St Pancras, which serves the Eurostar services, this part of the station is very downmarket.

Above and opposite: Two very different liveried HST power cars pictured at Doncaster on the beautifully sunny 26 October 2016. Above shows 43050, which is on loan from East Midland Trains heading north at 11.31, and opposite at 14.40 43274 *Spirit of Sunderland* is speeding south with Trans Pennine 185 120 on the left waiting to depart for Cleethorpes.

A Kings Cross-bound Virgin HST gets the right-away signal from a member of the platform staff at Doncaster on 26 October 2016

East Midlands 43082 *Railway Children* is waiting to make its next journey north at Kings Cross on 7 February 2017. This power car was on hire to Virgin to ease a temporary motive power shortage.

Above and below: Two views taken at Kings Cross of the line-up of trains during their layover. Above, Virgin 43317 and East Midlands 43082, captured on 7 February 2017. Below, Grand Central 59912 and Virgin 43316 on 24 August 2017. Since the station refurbishment, the extra light coming through the new roof has been a huge improvement.

Above and below: Two pictures taken on 24 August 2017 at the completely rebuilt and electrified Reading station. Above, 43003 *Isambard Kingdom Brunel* waits to depart with a westbound service. Below, 43015 and 43197 are both Paddington-bound. Both trains look very smart in their Great Western blue livery.

43138 is seen at Didcot station waiting to depart with a Bristol service on 24 August 2017.

43014 *Railway Observer* has just paused in Salisbury station at the rear of the Network Rail Measurement Train on its way to Exeter. 24 August 2017.

Express Diesel Trains

Closely watched by the gallery, 43300 *Craigentinny 100* speeds through Doncaster with the Kings Cross to Inverness Highland Chieftain service on 27 February 2019.

43318 heads north out of Doncaster in its special 'Celebrating 40 years of the Journey Shrinker' livery on 27 February 2019.

43302 arrives at Stevenage station with a Kings Cross to Leeds service on 3 June 2019. 43302 achieved a speed of 148.5 mph on 1 November 1987, making it the world's fastest diesel loco – a record it still holds today.

43300 *Craigentinny 100* departs from Doncaster with a train for Leeds on 3 June 2019.

43320 is stopped on the middle road at Doncaster alongside one of its its successors, 800 102, which will precede it on a service to Edinburgh. Although in this picture 800 102 is running on electric power, they are bi-modal and can run on their diesel engines on non-electrified lines.

Above and below: Two pictures taken at the open day held at Crewe Works on 8 June 2019. Both show East Midlands HST power cars in different liveries. Above, 43048 *TCB Miller MBE* in the original scheme. Below, 43423 *Valenta 1972–2010*, which has recently transferred from Grand Central in the latest version of the livery.

In 2019 Hull Trains were having problems with their Class 180 Adelante trains and had to borrow two sets of HSTs from Great Western, one of which, 43023 *SQN LDR Harold Starr*, is seen at Hull station on 21 September 2019.

CrossCountry 43321 is seen arriving at York with an Edinburgh to Plymouth train on 21 September 2019.

Not long after their introduction, Super Voyager 220 034 and 220 021 approach Ribblehead station on 23 February 2002 with a CrossCountry service diverted from the WCML.

220 011 stands in York station with a northbound CrossCountry service on 31 March 2004. Each of the four cars in these trains are equipped with a 750 hp Cummins diesel engine and have a maximum speed of 125 mph.

220 034 calls at Derby station with a Newcastle to Bournemouth service on 22 April 2006.

221 115 climbs towards Birkett Tunnel on the Settle & Carlisle with the 11.38 Glasgow to Plymouth service on 29 April 2006. This train was diverted because of engineering work on the WCML.

220 021 waits to depart from Carlisle station with a service for the West Country on 16 August 2006.

221 125 is seen at Oxenholme with a Glasgow to Paignton service on 1 September 2006.

221 123 arrives at Leeds with a northbound CrossCountry service on 9 May 2007.

It's pouring with rain in the distance, but up here at Birkett Common the sun shines on a Class 221 as it climbs to Ais Gill summit on 12 May 2007 with the diverted 11.45 Glasgow to Plymouth train.

Above and below: Two pictures taken on days when the WCML was closed for major works and all trains were diverted over the Settle & Carlisle. Both show two Class 221s working the 07.30 Penzance to Glasgow service. Above, it is seen just after it had passed through Birkett Tunnel on 12 May 2007. Below, just north of Kirkby Stephen, another pair of 221s just squeeze into the picture on 2 June 2007.

220 011 waits departure time at Darlington with an Edinburgh to Plymouth train on 17 September 2007.

220 021 arrives at Carlisle station with a Glasgow to Bristol service on 19 September 2007.

A Class 221 rides the curves through Low Gill with the Glasgow to Penzance train on 25 September 2007.

Further north that afternoon, 221 111 leans into another curvaceous stretch of track as it speeds down from Shap Summit and passes through Greenholme on its way to the West Country.

220 020 comes to a halt in Penrith station with a service for Glasgow on 29 September 2007.

221 123 waits to depart from Weston-super-Mare station with a Plymouth service on 29 February 2008.

On a wintery 7 February 2009, 221 103 heads north through Appleby station with a diverted train for Glasgow.

221 113 passes Causey Brow, and approaches Appleby station through the spring blossom with another diverted service for Glasgow on 21 May 2011.

The beautiful Brunel-designed Bristol Temple Meads station looks its best in the winter sunlight. This view was on 1 March 2008. On the left, 143 611 is about to leave for Bristol Parkway, while 220 018 will depart in the opposite direction to Taunton.

On a sunny morning at Manchester Piccadilly, 220 024, on the left, waits to depart for Bournemouth, while on the right another 220 will soon depart for Paignton. 25 May 2009.

A northbound 221 speeds through Tebay on 20 June 2009. This once busy junction for the line across the Pennines to Darlington closed completely in 1967 along with the loco depot. The black building above the last coach is the Junction Hotel (now flats), which was much loved by enthusiasts who stayed there in the last years of steam.

With the Eden Valley and the North Pennines in the background, 221 002 climbs towards Shap Summit through Little Salkeld with a southbound train on 20 June 2009.

221 115, with a Bombardier vinyl, passes through Little Salkeld just south of Penrith, with a train for Glasgow Central on 25 January 2014.

220 021 passes through Levenshulme station with a XC Manchester Piccadilly to Bournemouth service on 31 May 2019.

220 023 passes the very distinctive Heaton Chapel and Heaton Moor station with a XC service bound for Manchester Piccadilly on 31 May 2019.

220 001 calls at Doncaster on its way to Newcastle on 4 December 2014.

Virgin 221 101 is seen at the Crewe Open Day in its new livery. 8 June 2019.

An unidentified Virgin 221 is seen arriving at Crewe station on 9 June 2019 on a service to Glasgow. This picture, taken on platform 11, shows that the station's nineteenth-century buildings have survived with most of the brickwork in remarkably good condition.

Above and below: Two pictures of First Great Western Class 180 Adelante diesel-hydraulic trains, both taken on 3 June 2004. Above, 180 104 arrives at Reading with a train from Worcester to Paddington. Below, 180 114-106 at Paddington are ready for departure.

Three pictures of Hull Trains Class 180 Adelante trains in Hull station. Above and middle, 180 113 departs for Kings Cross with the midday service on 28 October 2014. Below, 180 109 waits for its afternoon departure.

180 109 arrives at
Doncaster with the
09.48 from Kings Cross
on 7 July 2015.

180 110 waits for
departure from
Doncaster on
14 February 2016 with
the 13.48 to Kings
Cross.

180 109 stands in Kings
Cross station having
just arrived with the
10.33 from Hull on
17 August 2016.

180 110 runs into Doncaster with the 09.48 from Kings Cross on 26 October 2016.

180 106 departs from Bolton station with a Northern Rail service from Blackpool to Manchester Victoria on 23 August 2011. NR had three sets of 180s from 2008 until 2011.

Grand Central 59907, part of set 180 107, stands at Doncaster while working a Kings Cross to Bradford service on 4 December 2014.

180 112 speeds north through Doncaster with a Grand Central Kings Cross to Sunderland service on 27 February 2019.

GC 180 114 rushes through Stevenage station on 3 June 2019 on the last leg of its journey from Sunderland to Kings Cross.

180 104 heads south through Doncaster on 3 June 2019 with a Sunderland to Kings Cross service.

An almost brand new 222 013 Meridian Midland Mainline train stands in York station with a service to St Pancras on 12 February 2005. This service operated on Saturdays only for a short period.

Seen on one of its more normal routes, 222 017 waits at Derby to depart for St Pancras on 22 April 2006.

Standing under the low roof at St Pancras 222 004 waits to depart for Sheffield on 17 August 2016. After spending a vast amount of money rebuilding the old St Pancras and the Midland Hotel, the money must have run out when it came to the services up the old Midland Main Line to Sheffield. The revitalised St Pancras and the hotel are a credit to the railway industry, but it is a shame that the same standards did not apply to the rest of the station.

At the other end of the line, 222 021 soaks up the sun at Sheffield station while waiting to leave for St Pancras on 17 August 2016.

Brand-new Azuma trains. Above, just out of the factory, 800 102 is running trials and passes through Doncaster on 27 February 2019. Below, 800 103 departs from York on its diesel power on 19 March 2019.

800 035 waits in Cardiff station with a service for Paddington on 23 July 2018. These units have now taken over most Great Western services from HSTs. They are bi-powered and here at Cardiff they will run on diesel power, but from Swindon onwards will run on overhead electric.

Hull Trains has also joined the Class 800 revolution, and their 800 302 is seen at Hull station soon after arrival from Kings Cross on 8 February 2020.